Stratad Theory

Precise Qualitative Research Methodology

by

Antony Last

Published by

Stratad Theory (Pty) Ltd
Somerset West
South Africa
7130

Copyright & Edition

Copyright © 2018-2024 by Antony Last

First Edition—December 2022

Second Edition—January 2023

Third Edition—April 2024

Fourth Edition—May 2024

Author correspondence

antonylast@gmail.com

Dedication

Dedicated to all researchers looking for methodological clarity and precision.

Although the researcher may recognise similarities between Stratad Theory and grounded theory, Stratad Theory is not a capture, remodelling, or renaming of grounded theory. Believing this would be akin to qualitative data analyst misunderstanding of classic grounded theory (cf. Glaser, 2005).

Stratad Theory is the egression of something new.

Contents

Foreword

It is with great pleasure and awe that I write this introduction to Last's latest book.

In my opinion, the Stratad Theory method is one of the upcoming methods of theorizing. This is the 4th theorizing method I have had the good fortune to read. Other than Glaser and Strauss (the originators of the grounded theory method), there are Richard Swedberg (The Art of Social Theory) and Shoemaker et al. (How to Build Social Science Theories) who lay down methods for theory development. The latter two do not name their methods but they provide some steps that a researcher can take for theorizing.

Last writes with an easy-to-read style. He provides examples that amply explain a particular strategy. He blends references as old as 200 years (1822) with the latest. This in itself can be seen as a refreshingly subversive act as international academia generally shuns references older than 30 years. I invite scholars to read Stratad Theory and use it to understand social issues. I, for one, will be using it for sure!

Shehr Bano Zaidi, PhD

May 2024

Preface

During my use of classic grounded theory, since 2018, in several studies ranging from land acquisition, tax, terrorism, policing, etc., to interpersonal (Last, 2020) and physical violence against women, I discovered and confirmed that there were potentially serious shortcomings in the grounded theory methodology (cf. Dudovskiy, 2021).

I came to the realisation that grounded theory, classic, constructivist, or otherwise, could be inaccurate and subject to the very conjecture and preconception Glaser (1978, 1998, 2005) incessantly gainsays.

This is not to say that all grounded theories, including my own, or all of their content, was bad.

I had in any event progressively utilised more and more of the newly arisen Stratad Theory principles which actually ground and integrate better than grounded theory.

I had kept meticulous notes on the manner in which I proceeded in each study, to analyse, arrange, and present each theory.

The time came when such information needed to be shared to offer a more precise qualitative research methodology.

This book is a synthesis of that information.

'Footnotes' throughout this book are given in-line, by asterisk (*), exemplified below, to accommodate publishing requirements.

Stratad Theory* uses its own vocabulary to specify exactly what it does.

* Besides 'Stratafication Theory', the following: 'Stratafied Theory', 'Stratid Theory', and 'Stratad Theory' do not appear in the literature, except the latter in my other works. 'Stratification theory', though, for example, in Clerk (1910) and Adkins and Vaisey (2009), is a specific theory, respectively, of combustion engine thermodynamics and societal demographics, and is not a research methodology. 'Stratified theory' (e.g., Almeida et al., 2017) may refer to information / conceptual classification, but not as specifically in research methodological idea naming.

Even where certain procedures appear similar in some respects to grounded theory, they differ, so that Stratad Theory does not use grounded theory vocabulary, because it is doing something different, and grounded theory vocabulary can be abstruse, misleading, and lacking in several respects, resulting in less than adequate theorising.

"Stratad Theory is seen as a more authentic form of theory generation" (Last, 2020, p. 327).

Sincerely,

Antony Last

Somerset West

18 May 2024

Introduction

Stratad Theory is named after the *natural* information *strata* found in data from which a theory can be built up into various *strata* of ideas.

There are many issues with grounded theory that could be explained and academically shown with exhaustive citations to be flaws and drawbacks, such as, sidelining accuracy (e.g., Glaser 2002b), scorning verification (e.g., Thulesius, 2019), plagiaritive coding (e.g., Glaser, 1965 from Boise, 1883 et al. (*n* = 12); Glaser, 2002a from Lazarsfeld, 1939)*, main concern confusion (e.g., Schurch, 2015), faulty core categories (e.g., Glaser, 2014), participant non-citation and speculative (forced) theoretical coding (e.g., Glaser & Strauss, 1965), hamperative impressionistic hand sorting, and premature category and memoing salience.

* Also, *fluctuating* as a theoretical term was suggested to Judith Holton by Barney Glaser, confirmed in her email of 9 June 2003 (Glaser & Holton, 2005, p. 14), in his 'flash of brilliance' phrase "fluctuating networks". Holton (2006) does not appear to acknowledge this in her thesis.

However, that is not the purpose of this book, and such an exposé must be left for another occasion.

In any event, this book is also not written as a replacement manual for grounded theory or any other qualitative data analysis methodology, although, in light of its comprehensive simplicity, some may take it as such.

Criticism will no doubt arise from the ranks of the Glaserian faithful, but to them be it said that an irrational adherence to something in which you have a stake is not sufficient reason to maintain it, and is in fact paradoxically against the spirit of openness ostensibly espoused and encouraged by Barney himself (Glascr, 2005). Now is the time to be open to the weaknesses of grounded theory, classic or otherwise, and to aspire to something better.

Here, the reader can expect to find a clear easy-to-follow methodology, laid out in seven succinct chapters, which will help in precise analysis, idea and function naming and arrangement, and theory building and writing.

In the chapters that follow, I will utilise fictitious data (made up by me) for the purposes of explaining how Stratad Theory does what it does.

Also, where I have cited thus "cf.", I similarity sourced and associated the item to illustrate ideas literally, metaphorically, or lexically, after I had written my Stratad Theory of Stratad Theory as you have it in this book, and therefore, in those instances, do not show quotations marks, as I am not quoting the sources but referring to them for related phraseology. However, I am not claiming use originality of term or phrase, except where the reference and the literature in general do not use it in relation to research methodology, which is most of the time.

Thank you very much.

Enjoy!

Chapter 1
Realistic Naming

Chief Issue and Central Solution

When analysing and **realistic naming*** (cf. Yasinetskaya, 2015) data in a study (to be shown below), you must constantly be asking yourself the following two questions.

* The names of all seven main principles / steps in Stratad Theory (as per the chapter titles in this book) arose naturally in their application. None were hijacked from other sources, although they may appear there (as referenced here by "cf."), but not relating to research methodology as far as can be determined.

1. What is the *chief issue* (cf. Whiting, 1868) in the data (for this study)? In other words, if

you are studying health carer communication, you are looking for signs of the *chief issue* for health carers in their communication with the carees—patients, frail persons, etc. If you are studying frail person communication, you are looking for the *chief issue* frail persons face in their communication with health carers, or others in general, depending on the scope of the study. Do not speculate about the *chief issue*. It must be generally apparent and *arise naturally* from the **realistic naming** of the *ideas* in the data.

2. The second question to be constantly asking yourself whilst **realistic naming**, is: What is the *central solution* (cf. King, 1938) to the *chief issue* (in this study)? As the *chief issue*

arises, tentatively or not, you can be on the lookout for ways in which the data might show its *solutioning** (how it is solved). Why? Because the purpose of any research endeavour is to find solutions to problems—a *central solution* to a *chief issue*. Once the *central solution* has arisen from data **naming** (cf. Plagman & Altshuler, 1972), you can *similarity source* (Chapter 6 below) to expand its explication.

*This term first appears in the literature referring to problem-solving in Webb's (1999) book *The Educator's Guide to Solutioning. The Great Things That Happen When You Focus Students on Solutions, Not Problems*, but is prompted for my use here by Guajardo, (2004b) of whose study I have been aware for some time now. It is both interesting and disturbing to note Guajardo's

(2004a, 2004b) apparently complete non-reference to Webb (1999), despite the close foundational similarity (cf. Glaser, 1978, p. 138) in the use of *solutioning* in education. Our use of *solutioning* in Stratad Theory, however, has essentially nothing to do with grounded theory.

But let's not jump ahead of ourselves. Let us look at the first important principle in applying Stratad Theory.

Naming Ideas Realistically

When writing theory, you want to be able to express the *ideas* and meaning of the data in general terms. This is taking data on a basic *stratum* (cf. Jones, 1854; Green, 1887) and placing it up on a more elevated *stratum* (cf. Wartmann & Quetelet, 1837) ideationally (cf. Von Gernet, 2014).

For example, if the data reads "I stood by his bed and waited for him to swallow his tablets", you might **name** the *ideas* (actions) in this data as *standing*, *waiting*, and *swallowing*. This is **realistic naming** which is realistic and precise (cf. Holling, 1964) because you have used the exact word roots appearing in the data to **name** the *ideas* (cf. O'Callaghan, 1971), adding -*ing*, the gerund (noun-verb) suffix.

You have also elevated these *ideas* to a higher *stratum*, because now *standing*, *waiting*, and *swallowing*, as *ideas*, no longer necessarily relate to "I", the study participant, or "him", whoever that might be, a patient, or other male person, depending on the study context. But exactly who the people are might not be relevant any longer, as more and more data is **realistically named**.

When **realistic naming**, do not use the exact form or order of the data words, thus avoiding plagiarism. For example, if the data states "I find I am always running quickly away… ", *running away* is good **naming**, but if you prefer 'running quickly', you should show it for its first appearance, at least, as "running quickly" with the anonymous participant or literature citation, whatever is applicable, and thereafter as *running quickly*. Always acknowledge your sources (cf. Fitzgerald, 1994).

So, a good way to manage **realistic naming** is to do so in an Excel or Google Sheet.

Programs like NVivo are not suitable for detailed **realistic naming**, as they only provide a limited number of themes which may not be relevant to the *chief issue* of your study and its *solutioning*. Also **naming** on sheets or scraps of paper or card (cf. King, 1844) is not realistic when it comes to manageability.

You start in the middle of a sheet (Google or Excel) at the top, entering a few column titles in the first row (which you freeze for scrolling purposes, e.g., View > Freeze > 1 row), and proceed with the **naming** beneath that, something like this:

realistic name	data	source
standing	I stood by his bed and waited for him to swallow his tablets	Participant 1
waiting	I stood by his be	Participant 1
swallowing	I stood by his be	Participant 1

Now, because things happen before and after **named** actions, we insert a <u>before</u> and <u>after</u> column, and enter into them what happened before and after (This helps with **concatenated arrangement**, **functional naming**, and **narratival delineation** later on. It also prevents fanciful or 'creative theoretical ordering' of ideas.):

before	realistic name	after	data	source
-	standing	waiting	I stood by his bed and waited for him to swallow his tablets	P. 1
standing	waiting	swallowing	I stood by his be	P. 1
waiting	swallowing	-	I stood by his be	P. 1

You will notice that "Participant 1" has been abbreviated to "P. 1". In the next snippet we have unwrapped the first data line and let it remain in its field like the others for reference purposes for double-clicking in the sheet field as one works. Also, if your data are literature items, then under <u>source</u> you would put the full reference.

Let's continue a bit, and **realistically name** some more data, e.g., "I stood at the door and waited for the family to say goodbye to her" (P. 2) and "I asked her if she was comfortable and waited for her answer. She nodded yes" (P. 3):

before	realistic name	after	data	source
-	standing	waiting	I stood by his	P. 1
standing	waiting	swallowing	I stood by his	P. 1
waiting	swallowing	-	I stood by his	P. 1
-	standing	waiting	I stood at the	P. 2
standing	waiting	saying goodbye	I stood at the	P. 2
waiting	saying goodbye	-	I stood at the	P. 2
-	asking	being comfortable	I asked her if	P. 3
asking	being comfortable	-	I asked her if	P. 3
-	waiting	answering	I asked her if	P. 3
waiting	answering	nodding	I asked her if	P. 3
answering	nodding	-	I asked her if	P. 3

You can colour-code / shade the repeating **names** (*ideas*) for visual effect—you don't need to do this, and you will shortly see why. Such colour-coded / shaded **realistic names** (e.g., *standing* and *waiting*; we add *asking*) indicate <u>participant</u> action, whereas the other actions under the **realistic name** column indicate actions of <u>others</u>. So, by *matching* and *contrasting* (cf. Burke, 1941), likeness and distinction (cf. Mitchell, 1912) are taken into account in the *arising* **names** (*ideas*) (cf. Lange, 1894).

Now in order to illustrate the subject of the next chapter, **Chapter 2: Concatenated Arrangement**, we will consider one more made-up data bit for **realistic naming** first thing in the next chapter and then show you what **concatenated arrangement** actually means.

Chapter 2
Concatenated Arrangement

Here is that data bit:

"I asked him if I could hand him the glass to drink some water. I waited. Eventually he said yes."

Meaning

Before we **realistically name** this data bit's *ideas*, what does **concatenated arrangement** (cf. Carpenter, 1840) mean?

'Catena' is the Latin word for 'chain', so 'catenated' means 'chainlike', and 'concatenated' means 'linking like a chain'.

And what is a chain? It is an arrangement of links all of the same type.

So **concatenated arrangement** simply means the linking together of the same or same type of **named** *ideas*, e.g., all the occurrences of *waiting*.

More Realistic Naming

Here is that data bit again: "I asked him if I could hand him the glass to drink some water. I waited. Eventually he said yes" (P. 4).

Let's **realistically name** the above data bit, then **concatenated arrangement** will become clear to you.

Note, for the purposes of this book, so that we don't shade too dark beyond visibility, we have enrectangled the occurrences of *answering* with a dotted line. *nodding* and *saying yes* are essentially the same concept, and so they are enrectangled with a solid line to show this.

before	realistic name	after	data	source
-	standing	waiting	I stood by his	P. 1
standing	waiting	swallowing	I stood by his	P. 1
waiting	swallowing	-	I stood by his	P. 1
-	standing	waiting	I stood at the	P. 2
standing	waiting	saying goodbye	I stood at the	P. 2
waiting	saying goodbye	-	I stood at the	P. 2
-	asking	being comfortable	I asked her if	P. 3
asking	being comfortable	-	I asked her if	P. 3
-	waiting	answering	I asked her if	P. 3
waiting	answering	nodding	I asked her if	P. 3
answering	nodding	-	I asked her if	P. 3
-	asking	handing	I asked him if	P. 4
asking	handing	drinking	I asked him if	P. 4
handing	drinking	-	I asked him if	P. 4
-	waiting	answering	I asked him if	P. 4
waiting	answering	saying yes	I asked him if	P. 4
answering	saying yes	-	I asked him if	P. 4

Alphabetical Ordering (cf. Cooper, 1916)

And now we **arrange** (Data > Sort range > Advanced range sorting options > Data has header row > Sort by realistic name A to Z >

Sort, in Google Sheets) this portion of the sheet alphabetically (cf. de La Cadena, 1872) by the **realistic name** column, and remove the colours / shades / rectangles as they are no more necessary for our discussion:

before	realistic name	after	data	source
waiting	answering	nodding	I asked her if	P. 3
waiting	answering	saying yes	I asked him if	P. 4
-	asking	being comfortable	I asked her if	P. 3
-	asking	handing	I asked him if	P. 4
asking	being comfortable	-	I asked her if	P. 3
handing	drinking	-	I asked him if	P. 4
asking	handing	drinking	I asked him if	P. 4
answering	nodding	-	I asked her if	P. 3
waiting	saying goodbye	-	I stood at the	P. 2
answering	saying yes	-	I asked him if	P. 4
-	standing	waiting	I stood by his	P. 1
-	standing	waiting	I stood at the	P. 2
waiting	swallowing	-	I stood by his	P. 1
standing	waiting	swallowing	I stood by his	P. 1
standing	waiting	saying goodbye	I stood at the	P. 2
-	waiting	answering	I asked her if	P. 3
-	waiting	answering	I asked him if	P. 4

Now we manually **arrange** (Insert rows > Cut & Paste, etc.) the rows by *priority* (*names* appearing more frequently), *salience* (*names* relatedly more important), and/or *natural order* (cf. Curson, 1702), not "hopeful… natural order" as in Glaser (2005, p. 192), or speculative or 'creative' theoretical sequence, thus:

before	realistic name	after	data	source
-	standing	waiting	I stood by his	P. 1
-	standing	waiting	I stood at the	P. 2
(standing)	asking	being comfortable	I asked her if	P. 3
(standing)	asking	handing	I asked him if	P. 4
-	waiting	answering	I asked her if	P. 3
-	waiting	answering	I asked him if	P. 4
standing	waiting	swallowing	I stood by his	P. 1
standing	waiting	saying goodbye	I stood at the	P. 2
(saying yes)	handing	drinking	I asked him if	P. 4
waiting	answering	nodding	I asked her if	P. 3
waiting	answering	saying yes	I asked him if	P. 4
answering	nodding	-	I asked her if	P. 3
answering	saying yes	-	I asked him if	P. 4
asking	being comfortable	-	I asked her if	P. 3
handing	drinking	-	I asked him if	P. 4
waiting	saying goodbye	-	I stood at the	P. 2
waiting	swallowing	-	I stood by his	P. 1

The names above in brackets are implicit in the data.

Spend enough time studying the above sheet to fully absorb how it was **concatenatedly arranged** and what those implications might be. *Standing* occurs in *natural sequence* (as indicated in the data) before *asking, waiting,* and *acting*. Therefore, although *waiting* is ideationally more emphasised, so far, in the data, *standing* and *asking* are two important (*salient*) actions prior to that.

In this fictitious study of ours on health carer communication, for example (follow in the **realistic name** column in the sheet above), the carer *stands, asks,* and *waits* for a response, then *acts* appropriately. Note that the **realistic names** beneath the line are all contained in the

<u>after</u> column above the line, and *nodding* and *saying yes* are, too, by their inclusion in *answering*.

Removing Rows

Therefore, as we are studying (looking for), for example, health carer *chief issue* and *solutioning*, and not that of carees (the ones being cared for), we can relegate (move) the rows beneath the line lower down in the sheet, or duplicate the sheet as a backup reference, and delete those rows beneath the line in the main sheet, thus:

before	realistic name	after	data	source
-	standing	waiting	I stood by his bed a	P. 1
-	standing	waiting	I stood at the door a	P. 2
(standing)	asking	being comfortable	I asked her if she w	P. 3
(standing)	asking	handing	I asked him if I coul	P. 4
-	waiting	answering	I asked her if she w	P. 3
-	waiting	answering	I asked him if I coul	P. 4
standing	waiting	swallowing	I stood by his bed a	P. 1
standing	waiting	saying goodbye	I stood at the door a	P. 2
(saying yes)	handing	drinking	I asked him if I coul	P. 4

Using Sufficient Data

As you continue to add rows below these, by more **realistic naming** of *ideas* in the data, you essentially follow the same procedure laid out above, *matching* and *contrasting* **realistic names** and building up a volume of **realistic names**, until their *salience* (related importance), *priority* (number), and *natural order* start to reveal the *chief issue* for the participants and how they *solution* it. Depending on how much data you have to **name** or how big your study is, you may add another, for example, 70 to 250 lines, or more, or less, **arranging** (**concatenatedly**) as you proceed. Do not **name** data irrelevant to the purpose of your study (e.g., health carer communication).

We now take a look at **higher naming** in the following chapter.

Chapter 3
Higher Naming

There may be many other actions that the health carers do in our example.

More Realistic Naming

Their data may add **realistically named** *ideas* of *walking, listening, watching, stopping, acknowledging, confirming, gesturing, hesitating, refusing, explaining, pausing, encouraging, reassuring, medicating, injecting, dressing, feeding*, etc.

We will add several of these to our list in the **realistic name** column by *matching,* *contrasting*, *ordering*, and *arranging* to illustrate how **higher naming** works, and just imagine that there could be multiple occurrences of the new **realistic names**, and that all the other columns in our sheet are properly filled in.

Lower to Higher Naming

Refer to the sheet section on the opposite page.

Related terms prior to *asking* are grouped at the top and **higher named** *approaching*, which term may or may not appear in the data, but the *idea* does.

Asking, *gesturing*, and similar seemed still best to be clustered under *asking* on the **higher** level.

Pausing and *hesitating* are both aspects of *waiting*, and *waiting* is *waiting*, so *waiting* is good as a **higher name**.

Then there are *listening*, different aspects of *replying*, and resultant *actions* which of course are also varied.

higher name	before	realistic name	after	data	source
approaching		walking			
approaching		stopping			
approaching	-	standing	waiting	I stood by his	P. 1
approaching	-	standing	waiting	I stood at the	P. 2
approaching		watching			
asking	(standing)	asking	being comfortable	I asked her if	P. 3
asking	(standing)	asking	handing	I asked him if	P. 4
asking		gesturing			
waiting		pausing			
waiting		hesitating			
waiting	-	waiting	answering	I asked her if	P. 3
waiting	-	waiting	answering	I asked him if	P. 4
waiting	standing	waiting	swallowing	I stood by his	P. 1
waiting	standing	waiting	saying goodbye	I stood at the	P. 2
listening		listening			
listening		acknowledging			
replying		confirming			
replying		refusing			
replying		explaining			
acting	(saying yes)	handing	drinking	I asked him if	P. 4
acting		medicating			
acting		injecting			
acting		dressing			
acting		feeding			

So on the **higher** ideational *stratum*, we have *approaching, asking, waiting, listening,* *replying*, and *acting*. *Waiting* in the broader sense seems to be the manner of *solutioning* of a *chief issue* of *miscommunication* or the fear of miscommunication which the carer's would have if they are doing all of these things to avoid it.

Central Solution from Data Naming

Thus, it is apparent that *waiting* uses *approaching*, *asking*, *listening*, *replying*, and *acting* in order to achieve its goal of ensuring clear communication, thereby providing the *central solution* to the possibility of *miscommunication* (the *chief issue*).

Chapter 4

Structuralisation*

* cf. Van Nostrand, J. J. (1896), *The Formal Concept for the Student Only* for a general reference to this idea not directly related to research.

We have just shown above, how **higher naming** groups the **lower (realistic) names** onto a higher level (*stratum*) ideationally (stratafication; cf. Reynolds, 1890), allowing for the *arising of a chief issue* and *central solution*.

Stratafication in the Theory Structure

Stratad Theory now **structuralises** the *arisen ideas* by **name** and *strata* to provide a *structure* (in a new sheet), something like this, from our example data:

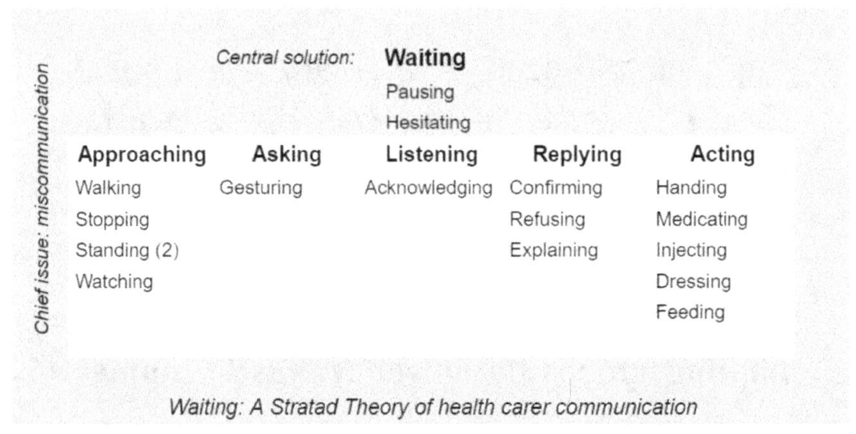

Waiting: A Stratad Theory of health carer communication

Central Solution from Structure

Waiting, the *central solution* to *miscommunication* uses *approaching*, *asking*, *listening*, *replying*, and *acting* to effectively *wait* to ensure clear and proper communication and action.

At this point, if it is clearly apparent, the study may be titled. In this instance, the title could be:

Waiting: A Stratad Theory of health carer communication

If we had enough **named** data in our example, there would be more **realistic names** and examples of **realistic names** under each **higher name** in our *structure* above.

Next we look at **functional naming**.

Chapter 5
Functional Naming

Functional naming (cf. Miles, 1964) is the **naming** of how the *arising* theory functions or appears to function as it *arises* over time of **naming** *ideas* in the data, both **realistic** (lower) and **higher**.

How the Parts Work Together
(cf. Poste, 1822)

For this we look to the data to see how the health carers in our example refer to their activities of *waiting, approaching, asking, listening, replying,* and *acting*. In this manner, you consider the possible sequential, static, or random (cf. Tömösközi et al., 2019) *vertical* and *horizontal stratafication* (cf. Newbold, 1850) of the activities.

The data may refer to these as steps, as in "the next step was for me just to listen", or skills, like in "I always am careful about my listening skills", etc. Participants may not actually mention any such elements.

Structure Study

This is where you will have to study the theory *structure* and decide what each element is and how it relates to each other as indicated in an overall manner by the data.

No guessing. It must be either explicit or implicit in the data (cf. McClintock, 1963).

Arising Functioning

In our example, it is feasible that the data suggest the **function** of *waiting* takes place through its **higher** *ideas* as *steps*, that each step's elements are viewed as *skills*, and that once the overall *solutioning* of *waiting* has ended on a particular occasion by performing the appropriate action (*acting*), there is a need for *timely checking* to take place, when *waiting* starts all over again on the next occasion by *approaching*.

Functionally Named Structure

The following *structure* is an example of how **functional naming** could *arise* from our example study:

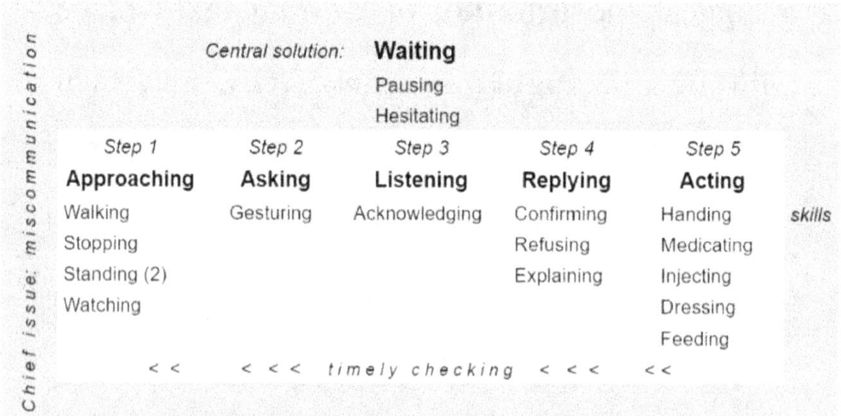

	Step 1	Step 2	Step 3	Step 4	Step 5	
	Approaching	**Asking**	**Listening**	**Replying**	**Acting**	*skills*
	Walking	Gesturing	Acknowledging	Confirming	Handing	
	Stopping			Refusing	Medicating	
	Standing (2)			Explaining	Injecting	
	Watching				Dressing	
					Feeding	

Waiting: A Stratad Theory of health carer communication

Waiting takes place through five *steps*. *Waiting* itself and its *steps* each have several *skills* which help to carry out its overall **function** and *steps* effectively and thoroughly.

Functional Statement (cf. Mead, 1904)

When *acting* has been done, *timely checking* requires that *approaching* will happen again in due course to ensure *waiting* does not start too late or unnecessarily soon.

Thus, **functional naming** is the naming of the *waiting* **function** which is *steps* and *skills* working together through *timely checking* to communicate properly.

Gaps in Theory (cf. Hinton, 1906)

As you build up your theory, you may find gaps, where, for example, you do not have sufficient occurrences of a specific **name** (*idea*), and you need to find more data on it.

Data Seeking (cf. Donnelly, 1965)

This is where **similarity sourcing** comes in.

Chapter 6
Similarity Sourcing*

* cf. Wermuth, et al. (2015) for the only other use of this term in the literature besides my own, but again not in relation to research methodology.

Searching in the Data

(cf. Walker, 1969)

You will now search (**similarity source**) in your data by keyword, related, or the same as your **realistic** or **higher name**, for which you need more occurrences (cf. Falaschi, 1990), and this is easy if your data is in a Google Sheet (Ctrl c, Ctrl f, Ctrl v), for example from a Google Form qualitative survey questionnaire, or you have simply entered your data in a sheet or document.

Obtaining Additional Data
(cf. Home, 1883)

Alternatively, you change some questions in your survey to obtain answers more specific to the *idea* in question, or ask such changed questions of your participants (cf. Egerer et al., 2018).

Adding to the Sheet and Structure

When you find the needed data, you **realistically name** it and **arrange** it in with your already *ordered* rows in your analysis sheet, and add any new **name** to the theory *structure* (cf. Berry, 1958).

Literature Sourcing

(cf. Guest, 1995)

You should also **similarity source** from the literature (e.g., keyword or similar search in Google Scholar and your own collection) to round out the needed *ideas*, showing the **data** bits and **sources** (e.g., Finke et al., 2008) in the appropriate columns of your analysis sheet.

Rotational Repetition

(cf. Barlow, 1901)

Repeat the activity of *searching in the data* and *literature sourcing, obtaining additional data*, and *adding to the sheet and structure* until the **named** *ideas* are sufficiently *infused* (cf. Sandifer, 1972)* with occurrences and meaning.

* Glaser (1978, p. 82) refers to analyst ideas being infused in more analyst ideas. This is not what is meant here. Here we are talking about **named** *ideas* having sufficient occurrences and meaning from the data to clearly show and illustrate the significance and operation of those *ideas*. Our use of infusion here is more akin to saturation in Glaser (2002a, p. 4).

Associating Ideas

(cf. Law, 1749)

The next step is the most exciting because this is where you associate the **named** *ideas* (cf. Mensch, 2019) together into a written theory.

This we cover in the next chapter on **narratival delineation**.

Chapter 7
Narratival Delineation

higher name	before	realistic name	after	data	source	notes
approaching		walking				Approaching t.
approaching		stopping				
approaching	-	standing	waiting	I stood by his	P. 1	
approaching	-	standing	waiting	I stood at the (	P. 2	
approaching		watching				
asking	(standing)	asking	being comfortable	I asked her if (	P. 3	
asking	(standing)	asking	handing	I asked him if	P. 4	
asking		gesturing				
waiting		pausing				
waiting		hesitating				
waiting	-	waiting	answering	I asked her if (	P. 3	
waiting	-	waiting	answering	I asked him if	P. 4	
waiting	standing	waiting	swallowing	I stood by his	P. 1	
waiting	standing	waiting	saying goodbye	I stood at the (	P. 2	
listening		listening				
listening		acknowledging				
replying		confirming				
replying		refusing				
replying		explaining				
acting	(saying yes)	handing	drinking	I asked him if	P. 4	
acting		medicating				
acting		injecting				
acting		dressing				
acting		feeding				

For example, in the sheet you make a **notes** column and start writing **notes** on the *ideas*, such as you can see the first one above starting 'Approaching…'. It actually reads '*Approaching* takes place through the paced and careful *skills* of *watching* and *walking* towards or past and back again to the caree, *stopping* and *standing* in close enough proximity so as to be personable and able to engage in communication (P. 1, 2)', citing all participants (anonymously) from whom the ideas were drawn. (Note: The additional intervening ideas in this statement should have *arisen* either from direct **names** or be implicit in the data. Again, no guessing, or ingenious manufacturing.)

Concatenated Noting

(cf. Jin et al., 2018)

Each sub-section and section of the sheet is written up in this manner with each note leading on to the next, so that you have a **narratival delineation** of the entire theory. You may intersperse it with appropriate direct quotes from the data properly cited, e.g., ' "I always listen carefully" (P. 19)' referring to the data from Participant 19, maintaining anonymity but preserving source integrity. If you quote from the literature or use the literature for a specific **named** *idea*, then show the citation as usual.

Copying to Word Processor

When the entire sheet is done, you copy and paste (Ctrl-Shift v) the **notes** column into Word or a Google Doc and there you have your first draft of the theory.

Reworking Drafts

Now you will need to work and rework the draft (cf. Housman, 1956) several times, improving it and knitting it all together (cf. Mitchell, 1973) in a coherent theoretical statement (cf. Creighton, 1899) over numerous pages, explaining how and under what conditions (cf. Wolpe, 1968), etc., the various *steps* and *skills* operate (cf. Fay, 1956) to achieve what they do, *waiting* to achieve *clear communication*, or stated more generally, *solutioning* to overcome the *chief issue*.

Epilogue

The first edition of this book was quickly followed by a second edition with tweaks as I have been pressured to get this information out so that researchers may start applying Stratad Theory.

The third edition removes colour coding and pictures to make publication less expensive and allow this book to be acquired by as many researchers as possible.

This fourth edition increases font and diagram size for ease of reading and application.

Other editions will follow as and when I receive feedback from readers concerning their questions and suggestions.

If you have any, please do not hesitate to email me at antonylast@gmail.com

I would love to hear from you.

Thank you,

Antony

References

Adkins, D. & Vaisey, S. (2009). Toward a Unified Stratification Theory: Structure, Genome, and Status Across Human Societies. *Sociological Theory. 27.* 99 – 121.

Almeida, J. P. A., Fonseca, C. M., & Carvalho, V. A. (2017, November). A comprehensive formal theory for multi-level conceptual modeling. In *International Conference on Conceptual Modeling* (pp. 280-294). Springer, Cham.

Barlow, W. (1901). I. Crystal symmetry. The actual basis of the thirty-two classes. *The London, Edinburgh, and Dublin Philosophical Magazine and Journal of Science, 1*(1), 1-36.

Berry, B. J. L. (1958). *SHOPPING CENTERS AND THE GEOGRAPHY OF URBAN AREAS. A THEORETICAL AND EMPIRICAL STUDY OF THE SPATIAL STRUCTURE OF INTRAURBAN RETAIL AND SERVICEBUSINESS.* University of Washington.

Boise, J. R. (1883). *Notes on Tischendorf's Text of Paul's Epistle to the Romans: With a Constant Comparison of the Text of Westcott and Hort*. University Press, John Wilson and Son.

Burke, K. (1941). Four master tropes. *The Kenyon Review, 3*(4), 421-438.

Carpenter, W. B. (1840). *Remarks on Some Passages in the Review of" Principles of General and Comparative Physiology" in the Edinburgh Medical and Surgical Journal, January 1840*. Philp.

Clerk, D. (1910). *The gas, petrol, and oil engine* (Vol. 1). Longmans, Green, and Company.

Cooper, L. (Ed.). (1916). *A Concordance to the Works of Horace* (Vol. 202). Washington: Carnegie Institution of Washington.

Creighton, J. E. (1899). Studies of Good and Evil. *The Philosophical Review, Vol. 8*, No. 1, pp. 66-69.

Curson, H. (1702). *The Theory of Sciences Illustrated: Or, The Grounds and Principles of the Seven Liberal Arts: Grammar, Logick, Rhetorick, Musick, Arithmetick, Geometry, Astronomy. Accurately Demonstrated and Reduced to Practice. With a*

Variety of Questions, Problems and Propositions Both Delightful and Profitable. R. Smith, London.

de La Cadena, M. V. (1872). *A Pronouncing Dictionary of the Spanish and English Languages...* Appleton.

Donnelly, M. D. (1965). Weyrauch: The Personality of Lawyers. *Michigan Law Review, 63*(6), 1128-1133.

Dudovskiy, J. (2021). *Grounded Theory: Disadvantages of Grounded Theory Methodology.* https://research-methodology.net/research-methods/data-collection/grounded-theory/

Egerer, M. H., Lin, B. B., & Philpott, S. M. (2018). Water use behavior, learning, and adaptation to future change in urban gardens. *Frontiers in Sustainable Food Systems, 2*, 71.

Falaschi, A. (1990). Automatic selection of phonologically compact phrases. *Le Journal de Physique Colloques, 51*(C2), C2-495.

Fay, L. C. (1956). *Reading in the High School. What Research Says to the Teacher # 11.* National Education Association, Washington, D.C.

Finke, E. H., Light, J., & Kitko, L. (2008). A systematic review of the effectiveness of nurse communication with patients with complex communication needs with a focus on the use of augmentative and alternative communication. *Journal of clinical nursing, 17*(16), 2102-2115.

Fitzgerald, M. (1994). Why write essays? *Journal of Geography in Higher Education, 18*(3), 379-384.

Gibby-Leversuch, R. (2018). *Dyslexia or literacy difficulties: what difference does a label make? exploring the perceptions and experiences of young people* (Doctoral dissertation, University of Southampton).

Glaser, B. G. (1965). The constant comparative method of qualitative analysis. *Social problems, 12*(4), 436-445.

Glaser, B. G. (1978). *Theoretical sensitivity*. Mill Valley, CA: Sociology Press.

Glaser, B. G. (1998). *Doing grounded theory: Issues and discussions*. Mill Valley, CA: Sociology Press.

Glaser, B. G. (2002a). Conceptualization: On theory and theorizing using grounded theory. *International journal of qualitative methods, 1*(2), 23-38.

Glaser, B. G. (2002b, September). Constructivist grounded theory? *In Forum qualitative sozialforschung/forum: Qualitative social research* (Vol. 3, No. 3).

Glaser, B. G. (2005). *The grounded theory perspective III: Theoretical coding.* Mill Valley, CA: Sociology Press.

Glaser, B. G. (2014). Choosing grounded theory. *The Grounded Theory Review, 13*(2), 3-19.

Glaser, B. G., & Holton, J. (2005). Staying open: The use of theoretical codes in grounded theory. *The Grounded Theory Review, 5*(1), 1-20.

Glaser, B. G. & Strauss, A. L. (1965). *Awareness of Dying.* Aldine Publishing Company, New York.

Green, W. L. (1887). *Vestiges of the Molten Globe, as Exhibited in the Figure of the Earth, Volcanic Action and Physiography.* E. Stanford.

Guajardo, M. G. D. H. (2004a). *'Solutioning': a model of students' problem-solving processes* (Doctoral dissertation, University of Warwick).

Guajardo, M. G. D. H. (2004b). Solutioning. *Grounded Theory Review*. Issue no.1, Volume 04.

Guest, G. S. (1995). *A tree for all reasons: the Maya and the 'Sacred' ceiba*. University of Calgary.

Hinton, C. H. (1906). *The fourth dimension*. S. Sonnenschein & Company, Limited.

Holling, C. S. (1964). The Analysis of Complex Population Processes1. *The Canadian Entomologist, 96*(1-2), 335-347.

Holton, J. A. (2006). *Rehumanising knowledge work through fluctuating support networks: a grounded theory.* (Doctoral dissertation, University of Northampton).

Home, D. M. (1883). Ben Nevis Observatory. *Nature, 27*(696), 411-411.

Housman, A. L. (1956). *The Working Methods of Sidney Howard*. The University of Iowa.

Jin, M., Bahadori, M. T., Colak, A., Bhatia, P., Celikkaya, B., Bhakta, R., ... & Kass-hout, T. (2018). Improving hospital mortality prediction with medical named entities and multimodal learning. *arXiv preprint arXiv:1811.12276*.

Jones, H. (1854). A manual of pathological anatomy. *The British and Foreign Medico-Chirurgical Review*, *13*(26), 369.

King, J. E. (1938). *Economic and social implications of the Southern Literary Messenger 1834-1864*. Honors Theses. 1101.

King, L. P. K. (1844). *A Selection from the Speeches and Writings of the Late Lord King*. London: Longman, Brown, Green, and Longmans.

Lange, K. (1894). *Apperception: A monograph on psychology and pedagogy*. DC Heath & Company.

Last, A. (2020). *Safetifying from interpersonal violence through Phasic Protective Sequencing: A classic grounded metatheory* (Master's dissertation). http://uir.unisa.ac.za/handle/10500/27146

Law, E. (1749). *Considerations on the state of the World, with regard to the Theory of Religion*. Cambridge.

Lazarsfeld, P. F. (1939). Interchangeability of indices in the measurement of economic influences. *Journal of Applied Psychology, 23*(1), 33.

McClintock, T. L. (1963). The Argument for Ethical Relativism from the Diversity of Morals. *The Monist, 47*(4), 528-544.

Mead, G. H. (1904). The relations of psychology and philology. *Psychological bulletin, 1*(11), 375.

Mensch, J. (2019). Embodied Cognition in Berkeley and Kant: The Body's Own Space. *Distributed Cognition in Enlightenment and Romantic Culture,* 74-94.

Miles, L. D. (1964). *History Of Value Engineering.* General Electric Company, New York.

Mitchell, A. (1912). The Presentation of Reality. *The Journal of Philosophy, Psychology and Scientific Methods, 9*(2), 50-54.

Mitchell, M. (1973). *Evaluation of the 1973 Summer Institute of the Ed. D. Program for Community College Faculty.* Nova Univ., Fort Lauderdale, Fla.

Newbold, C. (1850). Summary of the Geology of Southern India (Concluded from Vol. ix., p. 42). *The Journal of the Royal Asiatic Society of Great Britain and Ireland, 12*, 78-96.

O'Callaghan, D. (1971). The Meaning of Conscience. *The Furrow*, 78-86.

Orr, J. (1907). *The Bible Under Trial: Apologetic Papers in View of Present-day Assaults on Holy Scripture.* Marshall Bros.

Plagman, B., & Altshuler, G. (1972, January). An Integrated Corporate Data Base Concept and Its Application. In *Proceedings of 1972 ACM-SIGFIDET workshop on Data description, access and control* (pp. 395-420).

Poste, B. (1822). *Sermons* (Vol. 156). Paternoster Row, London.

Reynolds, C. B. (1890). *The Standard Guide, St. Augustine*. EH Reynolds.

Sandifer, C. M. (1972). *The Metamorphosis of Fiction: A Study of Methods and Techniques of Adapting Literature, and Especially Novels, to Readers Theatre*. Purdue University.

Schurch, L. S. (2015). *Seducing engagement: A classic grounded theory study of virtual leadership* (Doctoral dissertation, Walden University).

Thulesius, H. (2019). How classic grounded theorists teach the method. *Grounded Theory Review, 18*(1), 13-28.

Tömösközi, M., Luo, M., Fitzek, F. H., & Ekler, P. (2019, May). Initial Concept of an Oracle-Structured Stream Compression Protocol for Arbitrary Network Flows. In *European Wireless 2019; 25th European Wireless Conference* (pp. 1-6). VDE.

Van Nostrand, J. J. (1896). *The Formal Concept for the Student Only*. The author.

Von Gernet, A. (2014). Nicotian dreams: the prehistory and early history of tobacco in eastern North America. In *Consuming Habits* (pp. 81-101). Routledge.

Wartmann, M. M., & Quetelet. (1837). XXXII. Papers on the alleged periodical meteors of the 13th of November, and on shooting stars in general. *The London, Edinburgh, and Dublin Philosophical Magazine and Journal of Science, 11*(67), 261-273.

Walker, D. E. (1969, September). Computational linguistic techniques in an on-line system for textual analysis. In *International Conference on Computational Linguistics COLING 1969: Preprint No. 63*.

Webb, W. H. (1999). *The Educator's Guide to Solutioning. The Great Things That Happen When You Focus Students on Solutions, Not Problems*. Corwin Press, Inc., A Sage Publications Company, 2455 Teller Road, Thousand Oaks, CA 91320.

Wermuth, C. G., Villoutreix, B., Grisoni, S., Olivier, A., & Rocher, J. P. (2015). Strategies in the search for new lead compounds or original working hypotheses. In *The practice of medicinal chemistry* (pp. 73-99). Academic Press.

Whiting, W. (1868). *Address of Hon. William Whiting, Before the Boston Highlands Grant Club, August 5, 1868*. A. Williams.

Williams, T. (1875). *Mark Twain Sketches, New and Old*. The American Publishing Company, Chicago, Illinois.

Wolpe, H. (1968). A critical analysis of some aspects of charisma. *The Sociological Review, 16*(3), 305-318.

Yasinetskaya, N. A. (2015). THE LINGUAL AND STYLISTIC ESSENCE OF BORROWED ANGLICISMS. *Выпуск 1 (27) Языкознание*, 188.

Appendix
Stratad Theory Structure

As stated in the Introduction, this book contains my Stratad Theory of Stratad Theory.

Here is an expanded theory structure of Stratad Theory for your consideration, contemplation, and enjoyment:

Realistic Naming	Concatenated Arranging	Higher Naming	Functional Naming	Similarity Sourcing	Narratival Delineating
Issuing	Realisticing	Realisticing	Working	Searching	Associating
Solutioning	Ordering	Highering	Studying	Obtaining	Noting
Matching	Manualing	Ordering	Arising	Adding	Processing
Contrasting	Studying	Realisticing	Naming	Literacising	Working
Realisticing	Removing	Solutioning	Stating	Repeating	Reworking

Steps and *skills* had also *arisen* here (as in the example *waiting theory* above), but the reader must be aware that other *functional names* may also be applicable in the *arising* theories they produce. For example, in another theory, *functional names* could *arise* as *stages* and *skills*, *stages* and *steps*, or other completely different *names*.

Note the repetition, above, of *skills* for greater understanding of how inter-related they are in *repetitive rotating* to accomplish the goal of Stratad Theory (*stratad theorising*). This interpolation of certain *skills*, several times throughout, indicates the (*arising* from the data) need for balanced *repetition*. I have also written some *names* in a shortened form, such as *manual arrangement* as *manualing, realistic naming* as *realisticing, literature sourcing* as *literacising*, etc. This does not detract from their meaning contextually within the theory.

The data for my study resulting in this book on Stratad Theory are over 270 pages of exhaustive records of methodological procedures which I meticulously noted down as I worked on the production of over 11 theories.

Refer to the above structure: For Stratad Theory, the *chief issue*, in research methodology, was found to be *inadequacy* in doing the job of analysis and theory production properly. This was *centrally solved* by *stratad theorising* through the *structuralising rotational repetition* of *realistic*, *higher*, and *functional naming*, *concatenated arranging*, and *similarity sourcing*, until full *narratival delineation* was accomplished.

This resulted in Stratad Theory, a *precise qualitative research methodology*.